This book may be kept
SEVEN DAYS
A fine will be charged for each
day the book is kept overtime.

Dec. 5			
NOV 2 3 1993			

368.4
HOO

THE SOCIAL SECURITY SYSTEM

THE SOCIAL SECURITY SYSTEM

BY DOROTHY AND THOMAS HOOBLER

A GROLIER COMPANY

FRANKLIN WATTS
New York/London/Toronto/Sydney/1982
AN IMPACT BOOK

Photographs and cartoons courtesy of:
Culver Pictures, Inc.: p. 6;
United Press International: pp. 9, 25, and 35;
Rothco: pp. 15 (Ross), 40
(Copyright 1977 by Hy Rosen, The Times-Union),
and 51 (Mazzotta/Ft. Meyers News-Press, Fla.).

Library of Congress Cataloging in Publication Data

Hoobler, Dorothy.
The social security system.

(An Impact book)
Bibliography: p.
Includes index.
Summary: Examines the largest social program
in the United States primarily designed to meet
the income needs of retired and disabled workers.
1. Social security—United States
—Juvenile literature. [1. Social security]
I. Hoobler, Thomas. II. Title.
HD7125.H598 1982   368.4'3'00973   82-8347
ISBN 0-531-04490-4   AACR2

CONTENTS

THE SOCIAL SECURITY SYSTEM

INTRODUCTION

Social Security is the largest and most successful social program in American life. More than 93 percent of all Americans age sixty-five or over were eligible for benefits as of 1981. Each month in the second half of 1981 the postal service delivered $12 billion in checks to thirty-six million recipients. In addition to retirees, beneficiaries of the program include those of working age who are disabled and spouses and dependent children of retired, disabled, or deceased workers.

Benefits paid under the program increase with the inflation rate and are tax-free. They enable millions of elderly Americans to live with dignity and independence. Medicare, partially financed by Social Security, relieves participants of the crushing burden of spiraling medical and health-care costs. Families of participants in the program are guaranteed an income if the wage-earner dies or is disabled.

Social Security was conceived of as a pact between the generations to meet basic income needs. Rather than an insurance plan in the conventional sense, the system is a pay-as-you-go program that involves a direct transfer of money from active workers to those who are retired or disabled and to their families. The strength of the system depends on the confidence of those who are paying into it that the same benefits will be available to them when the need arises—in retirement, for instance, or in case of death or disability to his or her family.

Until recent years, Social Security was thought to be a sound concept. The program was politically popular, and its financial stability seemed assured. During the turbulent economic times of the 1970s, however, the stability of the program became a subject for widespread discussion and concern.

Congress approved great increases in benefits in the early 1970s and also tied benefits to the Consumer Price Index to make the program "inflation-proof." But the unexpectedly high inflation of the 1970s, along with rising unemployment and prices rising more rapidly than wages, put strains on the reserve funds of the system. Revenues went down as payments went up. Some analysts claimed that by sometime in the 1980s the system would not have sufficient funds to meet its payments.

Along with this short-range problem appeared the specter of a long-range threat to the system. The American birthrate has been declining, and improved health care and other factors have lengthened the overall life expectancy of Americans. These two developments created the prospect of fewer and fewer workers being required to pay for the benefits of more and more retirees. In 1950, sixteen workers were paying into the fund for each beneficiary. By 1981, the ratio of workers to beneficiaries was slightly more than three to one. Projections for the year 2025, when the "baby-boom" Americans born from 1945 to 1960 would have reached retirement age, indicated that the ratio might then be only two to one. Many people worried that the financial burden on tax-paying workers would be too great to bear.

In July 1981 a *New York Times* survey found that the majority of Americans under fifty years old did not believe they would receive full Social Security benefits. There was also growing resentment over the cost of the system to the average worker.

One-fourth of American families paid more in Social Security payroll taxes than they did in federal income tax.

Reform of the system loomed as a difficult and painful process. Politicians had always been glad to raise benefits, incurring the gratitude of the large number of retirees and other beneficiaries. But in mid-1981, when a newly elected and popular president, Ronald Reagan, proposed certain changes that would reduce benefit costs in the future, the furor that resulted caused him to temporarily shelve most of his plan.

Understanding the nature of the system—how it was planned and how it has grown—is central to deciding what changes are necessary to ensure its stability and solvency. Those who are paying into the system owe it to themselves to find out why it appears to be in trouble and what can be done about it. The Social Security system is complicated, for it has been built up over many years of legislation. But those who expect to benefit from it someday must now study its complex nature if they are to understand the dangers that face it today.

I

THE BIRTH OF
SOCIAL SECURITY

When Franklin D. Roosevelt became president in March 1933, the country was in the midst of the worst depression in its history. As Roosevelt took the oath of office, banks were collapsing, homes and farms were being repossessed because their owners could not pay mortgage payments, and there were about fifteen million people unemployed out of a total work force of about fifty million.

Former President Herbert Hoover had tried to deal with the so-called Great Depression by making federal loans to state and local governments to permit them to set up relief programs, and by asking private charities to help. Hoover's policies had been in the American tradition, which regarded public welfare as a local or state, rather than federal, concern. Because of the American tradition of rugged individualism, the United States had lagged far behind the European countries in passing social welfare legislation. By 1933, though, it was clear that traditional methods had failed on a massive scale. Roosevelt's New Deal programs were part of a greater willingness by the federal government to assume responsibility for the public welfare.

**This picture from the days of
the Great Depression shows an
unemployed worker selling apples
on the west side of New York City.**

The first hundred days of the Roosevelt administration were devoted to relieving those problems that demanded immediate attention. But in 1934, Roosevelt appointed the Committee on Economic Security to study long-range solutions to the problems of unemployment insurance, old-age insurance, and the general welfare; the chairman was Frances Perkins, the secretary of labor.

In the United States, old-age insurance had first been mentioned in the 1912 platform of the Progressive party. The Democratic platform of 1932, on which Roosevelt had run, pledged, "We advocate unemployment and old-age insurance under state laws." Roosevelt, the former governor of New York, had been one of the most important of the national leaders to urge social insurance.

Individually, the states had considered old-age pension plans from early in the twentieth century. In the 1920s eight states had passed laws setting up optional plans. More followed, but during the Depression the tendency had been to make such plans mandatory. In 1933 alone, ten states passed mandatory old-age pension plans, but they all paid benefits based on need. Coverage varied from state to state, and nearly half of the states still had no law at all.

The suffering of the Depression caused some people to urge drastic action to cure the nation's economic ills. Dr. Francis Townsend won wide support for his proposal to give all retired citizens aged sixty or over a pension of $200 a month, which they would be required to spend within thirty days. Elderly citizens would thus obtain immediate relief, and the spending requirement would pump money into a severely deflated economy.

Roosevelt felt the Townsend Plan was unworkable because the benefit amounts were so high (more than twice the average wage) and the eligibility age was so low.

One of Roosevelt's advisers later quoted him as saying: "The Congress can't stand the pressure of the Townsend Plan unless we have a real old-age insurance system, nor can I face the country without having devised at this time, when we are

[7]

studying Social Security, a solid plan which will give some assurance to old people of systematic assistance on retirement."

PASSAGE OF
SOCIAL SECURITY

The Social Security Act, which Roosevelt signed after congressional passage on August 14, 1935, was the most comprehensive piece of social legislation in the history of the United States. The law had three main areas of coverage.

First, it provided for immediate assistance of federal grants to the states to help them set up programs to aid dependent children and the blind and to provide maternal and child heath-care services, public health programs, and vocational rehabilitation. The act also included an unemployment insurance plan to be administered by the states, which were given the ability to determine their own standards for benefits.

Next, the program set up an Old-Age Assistance (OAA) program administered by the states and partially financed out of federal funds. Elderly citizens qualified for this program solely on the basis of need.

Most far-reaching in its effect was the program commonly referred to today as Social Security. This established monthly retirement payments that were to start in 1942 to retired workers aged sixty-five or over who had paid payroll taxes.

The amount of the monthly benefits was determined by the total amount of wages on which taxes had been paid, with a minimum monthly payment of $10. Persons who had not paid enough into the program to qualify for benefits, or the benefi-

FDR signs into law the Social Security Act. Behind him, in the dark suit, is Frances Perkins, the secretary of labor and chairman of the Committee on Economic Security.

ciaries of workers who died before reaching age sixty-five, would receive a lump sum payment.

The payroll taxes collected under this plan would go into a fund held by the government. Although the federal government would make no direct contribution, it would hold the fund and be responsible for administering it. The Social Security Board, an independent federal agency, was established for this purpose.

The payroll tax was to begin in 1937. Both employee and employer would pay 1 percent each. The payroll tax was to rise in stages of 0.5 percent every three years so that the rate for both employee and employer would reach 3 percent by 1949.

With the exception of railroad workers, who had their own retirement system under the Railroad Retirement Act, all employees in commerce and industry were covered by the tax. Among those exempt from the program were farm workers, self-employed professionals, and government employees. In all, about six out of every ten workers in the United States were covered by the plan.

Many features of the Social Security system served to make it a permanent, widely accepted part of American life. There was to be no "means test" for benefits; anyone who had paid a sufficient amount into the program could collect benefits after retirement. The benefits schedule was progressive; that is, those who had paid the least into the program received proportionately more than those whose wages and taxes had been higher. Benefits did rise with the amount of wages on which taxes had been paid into the plan, but those who had lower earnings or who were near age sixty-five at the start received a "better deal" than did those who were covered longer or at higher wages.

A basic part of the philosophy of the program was the method of financing it. The Committee on Economic Security had originally recommended a combined employee-employer payroll tax that would reach 5 percent around 1965. After that, general revenues of the government would be used to supplement the payroll tax in paying benefits. The committee reasoned that employees would not be able to pay more than 2.5 percent of their wages to the program, and employers required to pay above that level would probably reduce workers' pay accordingly. (In fact, as of 1982, the tax had reached 6.7 percent for both worker and employer.)

Roosevelt disregarded this recommendation of his committee. In the bill that was finally proposed, both employee and employer would each be paying 3 percent of payroll by 1949. (Since the mature program was projected as costing 10 percent, this would leave a shortfall of 4 percent.) Before this time, however, payments into the system would have produced a large reserve fund. The reserve funds were to be invested in interest-bearing U.S. government securities (bonds), and the interest could be used to supplement the payroll tax without the need for using general government funds.

Not everyone was pleased by this aspect of the program. In 1937, the influential Republican Senator Arthur H. Vandenberg attacked the planned accumulation of a reserve fund, estimated to reach $47 billion by 1980. Vandenberg said, "It is scarcely conceivable that rational men should propose such an unmanageable accumulation of funds in one place in a democracy." Other conservatives in Congress feared that Congress would fail to allot the excess revenues of the payroll tax to the reserve fund and, instead, would use them to liberalize benefits.

The payroll tax schedule that financed the system also drew criticism. The tax was regressive in that it took the same percentage (1 percent) of everyone's income, up to the level of $3,000 of annual earned income. A worker earning $100,000 paid the same as a worker earning $3,000.

Despite the regressive nature of the payroll tax, Roosevelt felt the program would be strengthened by having it directly financed through a tax earmarked for that purpose alone. Such a method of financing benefits created the impression that the benefits were a right that was earned by those who had paid into the system. The president remarked to one adviser, "I guess you're right on the economics, but those taxes were never a problem of economics. They are politics all the way through. We put those payroll contributions there to give the contributors a legal, moral, and political right to collect their pensions. . . .With those taxes in there, no damn politician can ever scrap my Social Security program." President Reagan, in the 1980s, would feel the truth of Roosevelt's prediction.

Continued criticism of the financing of the Social Security program led to the creation in 1937 of an advisory council that was to examine the arguments and decide on a final method of financing and benefits. Together with the Social Security Board and the president, the council drew up proposals to amend the original 1935 law. On August 10, 1939, amendments were passed by Congress that embodied some of those proposals.

RESULTS OF THE
1939 AMENDMENTS
The 1939 amendments drastically reduced the size of the future growth of the program's reserve fund, then named the Federal Old-Age and Survivors Insurance Trust Fund. The reduction was accomplished by making the system more of a pay-as-you-go program.

Benefit payments were scheduled to begin two years earlier than originally planned, and the increase in the payroll tax scheduled for 1940 was deferred. In addition, benefits were increased by paying them on the basis of a worker's average monthly wage, rather than on the total amount of wages on which a worker had paid tax.

Dependents of beneficiaries were now made eligible for benefits; for example, an aged wife and/or dependent child of a beneficiary was entitled to an amount equal to half of the basic benefit. Certain surviving relatives of a deceased beneficiary (widows over sixty-five; widows with children; orphans; dependent parents over sixty-five) were also made eligible to receive benefits, even though they themselves might not have paid any payroll taxes.

The amendments also strengthened the progressive aspect of the scale of benefits; that is, lower-income participants received a better rate of return in their retirement benefits than higher-income participants. The social needs of the Depression years prompted this change. Nonetheless, the program still remained primarily a middle-class plan.

In addition, the original money-back payments in case of death were eliminated, a small lump sum was substituted, and the lump-sum payment for those who paid taxes for too short a time to qualify was dropped. At the same time, it was made easier to qualify for minimum benefits. Finally, the federal grants to state programs for Old-Age Assistance were increased.

The 1939 changes were politically popular, because they increased benefits and paid them sooner without seeming to increase the costs of the system. Though the program favored the married over the single taxpayer (by granting benefits to nonworking wives and children), this caused few problems in an era when the norm was married couples with larger families than are common today.

But the changes only disguised the true costs of the system. There were many more workers who were paying into the system in 1940—the first year of benefits—than who were receiving benefits. The existence of the Old-Age Assistance program also disguised costs, since most elderly citizens in need of help received payment from this part of the program, which was not payroll-tax supported.

Some critics pointed out that as the system "matured," the number of beneficiaries proportional to taxpayers would rise. Few paid attention to these warnings. For the time being, payments were kept low, and most members of an elected government find it difficult to become concerned over a fiscal problem that may not arise for twenty years or more.

THE PLAN:
INSURANCE OR WELFARE?

In one kind of private insurance plan, participants pay small amounts over a long period of time to assure financial assistance in case of death, disaster, or retirement. The similarity between this and the payroll-tax-supported part of Social Security led to wide use of the term "Social Security insurance." As Roosevelt had predicted, the program became entrenched in the public mind as something that workers had paid into, and thus were entitled to benefit from. The American Federation of Labor supported the program, despite its regressive tax structure, because its leaders chose to see the payroll tax as an insurance premium that would produce benefits without the necessity for a means test.

Ironically, as the system expanded, the link between tax payments and benefits actually grew weaker; benefits grew without a corresponding rise in taxes. The program executives, who shaped the system, rejected both (1) a true insurance plan, in which the return would be closely related to investment, as in private insurance, and (2) a social program designed to help only those who could prove a need for it.

The program executives rejected the notion of adequacy, which would have concentrated benefits on the needy, because, as one of them stated, "a program for the poor is a poor program." They feared that a means test, in which a beneficiary would have to show financial need, would jeopardize support for the program among the middle class, whose payroll contributions provided the bulk of the program's funds.

If the chief beneficiaries had been only the poor, Congress might easily have lowered benefits when the funds were needed—for example, in 1981, when President Reagan wanted to balance the budget and increase defense spending. But the universal contributory system of the payroll tax bound office-holders. It increased the likelihood that the benefits would be paid as promised. It created an obligation that politicians could disavow only at the cost of political unpopularity.

"Did you see my Social Security application?"

If the program was not to be a welfare program, neither was it truly to be an insurance plan. In private insurance, a participant's payments are invested by the insurance company to produce an ever-growing fund that will be there when the insurance holder needs it to draw on. The 1939 amendments weakened the function of the original Social Security fund; those paying into the program were in fact directly paying the pensions of those who were collecting.

Another difference from a private insurance system was that Social Security benefits would not be paid until the recipient was actually retired. There was to be a ceiling on "earned income" that a recipient could have. Some argued that all recipients should be eligible for benefits at age sixty-five, whether they retired or not. The program executives argued that Social Security was not an annuity for the elderly but insurance against the loss of earning power.

COSTS OF
THE SYSTEM
Though politically popular, the hybrid system that combined insurance with welfare was not without its critics. Those on the left felt benefits should be higher. On the other side, some conservatives felt that dividing old-age assistance between OAA and Social Security only disguised the eventual costs. They wanted a universal program, with benefits paid to all and financed out of general revenues.

Milton Friedman, a conservative economist, criticized the hybrid system: "It gives too much attention to 'need' to be justified as return for taxes paid, and it gives too much attention to taxes paid to be justified as adequately linked to need."

Those who set up the system knew that if it had been paid from general revenues, there would have been an annual entitlement debate in Congress, setting the level of benefits. The symbolism of the payroll tax creating funds as needed was more attractive and fit in with American ideas of individualism.

Moreover, a system supported entirely by payroll taxes was thought to impose its own discipline by limiting expenditures to what taxpayers would tolerate. But the 1939 amendments—as some critics pointed out—produced a revenue surplus in the early years only because the ratio of taxpayers to beneficiaries was artificially high.

World War II extended the period of artificial revenue surplus because those workers who might have retired stayed on the job to take the places of young men in the armed forces. Additionally, many women joined the working force at home and began making their own payments into the Social Security system. After the war, the economic growth of the country further swelled the income derived from payroll taxes.

With continued surpluses in the amount of money collected by the system, the president and Congress faced the welcome task of setting benefit levels. Their choices seemed to fall into three categories: (1) benefits pegged to the prevailing average wage; (2) benefits that would provide an ideal standard of living; and (3) benefits that would provide a minimum subsistence level.

In the 1930s, the policy-makers made their choice with an eye to maintaining and expanding the program. First, Social Security benefits should be high enough so that "social insurance" rather than public assistance (OAA) would in the long term be the major program for the elderly. Second, benefits should be increased regularly. These decisions would have long-term ramifications.

2

THE SYSTEM EXPANDS

Conservatives who oppose the growth of the federal bureaucracy frequently complain that government programs, once established, seem to take on a life of their own. Certainly that has been true of Social Security. The whole history of the program has been one of expansion from its original, apparently modest, scope.

Expansion has come about in three ways: (1) by increasing the number of workers covered by Social Security; (2) by raising the amounts of both retirement benefits and payroll taxes; and (3) by creating new benefit programs in addition to the original old-age benefit program.

The growth of the program was not accidental. Those who administered it, and political leaders who supported it, consciously made the decisions that led to its expansion. From the beginning, the calculations that determined the amounts of basic benefits were very complicated. Only a small number of experts could understand them. Some of these experts administered the program; others were members of congressional committees that devised new legislation concerning the system.

One of the calculations the experts used was a type of economic projection called the level earnings estimate. It was a way of determining the amount of money that would be collected through the payroll tax. The level earnings estimate projected that average earnings would remain constant, or level. When, in fact, earnings rose in the post-World War II economic boom, it was found that there was more money in the Social Security fund than expected. This surplus was an incentive to persuade Congress to increase benefits and extend coverage of the system.

AMENDMENTS OF THE 1950s

When Social Security began making payments in 1940, it was a smaller program than the state-administered Old-Age Assistance program that was based on need alone. As late as 1949, OAA paid an average of 70 percent higher benefits than the average Social Security benefit. OAA also covered more beneficiaries. But the Social Security planners, mindful of the dictum that "a program for the poor is a poor program," were determined that the Social Security system would expand to include many of those who were otherwise eligible only for OAA.

A number of amendments to the Social Security law passed by Congress during the 1950s brought millions of additional Americans into the Social Security program. Eventually, virtually every employed American was either under Social Security, had a private pension plan, or was covered by a separate pension plan for government workers. The programs administered by OAA were eventually absorbed into Social Security or became part of the state welfare programs.

The amendments also made it possible for newly covered workers to achieve a "fresh start" in the program. The new law allowed them to qualify for benefits after they had paid the payroll tax for only a short time. In the future, full benefits would be paid to *all* workers who had participated in the program for a minimum time. Benefits were determined by the average salary that a worker had received and paid taxes on.

In addition, the amendments to the program during the 1950s increased the average monthly benefit from $43.86 in 1950 to $61.90 in 1955. These increases were justified by the rise in the cost of living from what it was in 1940, but they also weakened the equity of the system by making benefits less related to the amount of money a worker had paid into the system.

RAISING THE PAYROLL TAX

There was some recognition that the expanded program would require greater revenues—and a rise in taxes. The original plan of raising the payroll tax on both employees and employers by 0.5 percent every three years had been postponed several times, and in 1949 the tax was still the same as it had been in 1937.

Congress responded in 1950 by raising to $3,600 the wage base maximum on which taxes were paid. In the same year the tax rate increased to 1.5 percent each for both worker and employer. Congress passed a schedule of tax increases whereby the rates would rise to 3.5 percent each in 1970.

Even so, some people worried that in the long run the tax increases would not be enough to support the system. As early as 1943, one estimate had put the system in deficit in the long term by $16.5 billion. That seemed an impossibly large figure in those days, but Congress answered the possibility by agreeing that general revenues could be used to finance the system if the payroll tax proved insufficient.

However, Congress reversed itself in 1950, rejecting the use of general revenues to support Social Security on the grounds that to do this would be unfair to those persons not covered by the plan, that it would lead to a means test, and that opening the program in this way might lead to an unrestrained rise in benefits.

The amendments of the 1950s, in weakening the relationship of paid-in taxes to paid-out benefits, further weakened the comparison of Social Security to a private system of insurance. None-

[21]

theless, political rhetoric continued to identify the system as a form of old-age insurance, and in the public's mind, the right of a worker who had paid taxes to collect benefits was strengthened.

Not all politicians agreed. Conservative Republican Senator Robert A. Taft, during the debates on the 1950 amendments, said of the system: "It is not anything in the world but the taxing of people to provide free services to other people. . . . It is not insurance, and, at least up to [now], this system has not been very social either, because it has covered only a very small portion of the total number of people who are over sixty-five years of age."

DISABILITY ENTERS THE
SYSTEM OF BENEFITS

Dwight D. Eisenhower won the presidential election of 1952 by a large margin. He was expected to slow down some of the programs, including Social Security, that twenty years of Democratic administrations had established and expanded. Instead, the Eisenhower years saw the first major change in the scope of the Social Security program since 1939—coverage for disability.

Disability coverage began with a 1954 amendment to Social Security that provided for a "disability freeze." This protected workers from the loss of their ordinary benefit rights in case they were unable to work and thus continue to pay payroll taxes that would make them eligible for later benefits. The 1954 amendment also increased the wage base maximum to $4,200.

In 1956, another amendment provided for direct disability payments to those workers over fifty who were unable to work for a long time or permanently because of a mental or physical disability. The minimum age was later eliminated so that persons of all ages were eligible.

The same 1956 amendment also allowed women to retire at the age of sixty-two, although they would collect lower benefits than if they had waited until age sixty-five. The same privilege was extended to men in 1961. To pay for the increased benefits, the 1956 amendment increased the payroll tax by 0.25 percent for both employer and employee.

In 1958, more benefits were added to the disability program. The standards of eligibility were liberalized, and dependents of disability beneficiaries were made eligible for benefits of their own. The tax rate was increased from 2.25 percent to 2.5 percent for 1959.

Even though the wage base and tax rate had been raised several times, the increased revenues proved in the long run not to be enough to cover the costs of the new programs. Part of the problem was the difficulty in predicting the number of people who would become disabled. The numbers of people applying for disability payments turned out to be higher than the program's planners had expected. Opponents of the program argued that the existence of disability coverage actually encouraged more people to stop work because they knew they could receive disability payments. In addition, determination of a worker's eligibility for payments was left to state agencies, and standards varied.

Opening the program to include disability coverage was a major step toward the broad coverage that Social Security provides today. Furthermore, in going beyond the original purposes of the Social Security plan, disability payments made other types of coverage seem feasible. A more costly expansion of Social Security soon followed.

MEDICARE
The Social Security planners had long wanted to include health-care payments in the program. The original Committee on Economic Security under Roosevelt had looked into this possibility. Most other Western countries had some form of national health insurance, but in the United States the American Medical Association and other lobbies for doctors had long opposed such a

plan. To them it bore the taint of socialized medicine, which they claimed would reduce the quality of health care.

During the administration of President Lyndon B. Johnson, many new social programs were passed under the umbrella of The Great Society. One of these, enacted in 1965, was Medicaid, which provided health care for those who met a means test. Medicaid, though administered by the Social Security Administration, was paid for out of general revenues instead of payroll taxes.

Medicaid was a limited program, but along with it Congress authorized Medicare, which provided health-care insurance for Social Security beneficiaries aged sixty-five or older. As a result of amendments in 1972, it also gives benefits to people of any age with permanent kidney failure and disabilities that have lasted at least two and a half years.

Medicare is a two-part program. Part A is a hospital insurance program (HI) that helps pay for hospitalization costs and some kinds of follow-up outpatient care. Part B helps pay for doctor's fees and other medical items and services.

Part A of Medicare (HI) is financed through the Social Security payroll tax. Part B is voluntary. Those who wish to be eligible for benefits under Part B must enroll for it and pay monthly premiums, as in a private insurance program. The premiums of those enrolled under Part B are supplemented by general tax revenues of the U.S. government.

Medicare Part A, or HI, is different in at least one important way from the regular old-age retirement plan (OASI). There is no retirement test for HI. Hospital insurance starts automatically at age sixty-five for a covered worker, whether or

Lyndon B. Johnson signs into law the Medicare program. Next to him, standing, is Vice-President Hubert H. Humphrey and, sitting, former President Harry S. Truman.

not he or she is still working or is retired. This provision opened the way for many to collect HI benefits who would not otherwise have been eligible.

Another provision, passed in 1972, further widened the scope of the program to include all Americans, whether or not they had ever paid the Social Security payroll tax. Anyone could, and can today, buy the Medicare hospital insurance by paying a monthly premium. But to buy hospital insurance they must also pay premiums for the Part B medical insurance.

Medicare proved to be an enormously expensive program. When it was passed, there were warnings that the ultimate costs of the program would be very difficult to estimate. If the costs went too high, it was feared, they might jeopardize what was previously the major part of Social Security—the retirement benefits. Medicare was also a blow to equity in the system because Medicare benefits were not tied to what an individual participant had paid into the system.

Hospital costs soared in the years after Medicare was passed, mostly due to an inflated economy and expensive new technologies. Some argued that Medicare permitted the costs to rise to the degree they did. Without it, almost no one could afford to pay them. Medicare, so the argument went, permitted doctors and hospitals to prescribe tests and treatments that were of marginal value to the patient.

On the other hand, some of the supporters of Medicare claimed that it was not generous enough. Even with it, a truly catastrophic illness, requiring a long hospital stay, could destroy the savings of an elderly person and his or her family.

THE GREAT LEAP IN
SOCIAL SECURITY BENEFITS

Despite the warnings, increases in the Social Security system were politically popular. Between 1951 and 1971, Congress voted seven times for increases in benefits for both current and future eligible retirees. In small increments, the average monthly benefit more than tripled during these years.

These increases were partially paid for by increments in the tax rates. The increments seemed small in view of the potential benefits, and there was never enough resistance to the continuing rise in taxes to prevent Congress from passing them. The "level earnings assumption" also continued to make it seem that more money was coming in than expected, and thus made it reasonable for Congress to continue to pass benefit increases.

In addition, the system had still not fully matured. A worker who took a full-time job after graduation from high school at age 18 in 1937 would not turn 65 until 1984. It was not until that year approached that the full costs of the system would become apparent.

Meanwhile, the Medicare program of 1965 increased the tax rate to 4.2 percent and the wage base (the maximum amount of earnings on which the Social Security tax was levied) increased to $6,600. In 1968, old-age benefits were increased 13 percent and the wage base to $7,800. In 1969, benefits were increased by 15 percent (effective in 1970); in 1971, another 10 percent increase in benefits was approved and the wage base raised to $9,000. The tax rate by that time was 5.2 percent.

The greatest increase came in 1972. Ironically, it came during the administration of Republican President Richard M. Nixon. Nixon had little sympathy for social programs in comparison to his Democratic predecessor, but 1972 was a year in which he would be running for re-election. He proposed to Congress a 5 percent increase in old-age benefits.

The members of Congress, most of whom were running for re-election, were even more generous than Nixon. They were invited to be generous by Wilbur Mills, the chairman of the House Ways and Means Committee, who was himself planning a run for the presidency.

Mills was known to be one of the few people in Congress

who really understood the workings of Social Security; he was also regarded as a fiscal conservative. Thus, his opinion that a large rise in Social Security benefits was possible almost guaranteed its passage.

Mills, backed up by data from the Social Security Administration, argued that the level earnings assumption previously used for predicting how much money would flow into the system was too conservative. He backed a dynamic earnings assumption, which assumed that the economy would continue to grow and that wages would rise. This prediction was based on the economic experience of the country since World War II. But the application of it to Social Security meant that a very large rise in benefits was possible without the necessity for a corresponding increase in taxes.

Congress could hardly resist such a windfall in an election year. It passed a bill that raised the old-age benefits 20 percent. In addition, it provided for *automatic* increases in benefits and the wage base (maximum salary) on which taxes were paid. Beginning in 1975, benefits were to be tied to the Consumer Price Index, which is an average of selected prices.

In addition, Congress approved new methods for computing the primary old-age benefits, so that payments would start at a higher level than they had before. Congress also made it possible for eligible beneficiaries to collect benefits while having higher earnings than was permitted earlier.

To pay for all this, Congress merely raised the wage base to $10,800 for 1973. Nixon signed the bill.

Some voices had spoken out in opposition. John Byrnes, the senior Republican on the House Ways and Means Committee, told the House

At no point has there been a study by the Ways and Means Committee of the new method of financing that has produced the "windfall" that now is going to be used for the 20 percent benefit increases. Not one

word of testimony in public or executive session has been received on this subject. This fundamental change in the criteria by which the soundness of the Social Security trust fund has been measured for one-third of a century is being adopted willy-nilly by the Congress without even a cursory review.

It was not long before the effects would begin to be felt.

3

CRACKS IN THE SYSTEM

In 1973, government actuaries predicted that the Social Security System would have to dip into its reserve funds to pay the new benefits. The dynamic earnings level used to justify the 1972 increases had not proved accurate. Congress passed a quick fix in 1974 by raising the wage base to $13,200.

The rise in the wage base was not enough. As the decade went on, more predictions appeared showing Social Security to have a long-term deficit. Even in the short term, deficits began to appear. In 1975, the three trust funds—for old-age and survivors (OASI), disability (DI), and health insurance (HI)—declined by $1.5 billion. This was the amount by which benefits paid in that year exceeded tax revenues and interest on the funds.

For the first time, Social Security became a subject of real concern. People began to worry that when their turn came to receive benefits, there would not be enough money to pay them.

What had happened?

First, it is necessary to look once again at the methods used for predicting how much money would flow into the system. The level earnings assumption, used until 1972, projected that earnings—and hence tax revenues—would be "level," or remain about the same in the future. As earnings did, in fact, grow in most of the postwar years, there regularly appeared a surplus. More money was coming in than had been projected. Congress disposed of this money by raising benefits. But the surplus was only temporary. The surplus funds should have been saved for years when there was a shortfall of earnings taxes.

Neither liberals nor conservatives were happy with the level earnings assumption. Liberals felt that it kept benefits from rising because it failed to provide for the actual growth in the economy. Conservatives felt that it created the appearance of surpluses to justify increased benefits that would eventually prove too costly.

The adoption of the dynamic earnings assumption in 1972 seemed to reflect more accurately the true path of the economy. Wages *had* continued to rise, and so why not pay benefits on the assumption that they would go on rising?

In fact, the number of employed persons in the United States dropped from 1973 to 1974 and then dropped again very sharply the following year. Taxes that unemployed persons were "supposed to have" paid into the Social Security system did not appear.

The adoption of the dynamic earnings assumption could not have come at a worse time. Economic pressures from the underfinancing of the Vietnam War and the OPEC oil crisis of 1973 triggered the steep inflation of the 1970s. Deficit spending had gone on too long and risen too high. The great increase in oil prices after 1973 touched every segment of the economy.

The rise in prices triggered an inflationary spiral. Many union workers had contracts that called for an increase in wages as the Consumer Price Index rose. Prices caused wages to rise, and the rise in wages led to another rise in prices. Unfortunately, inflation in the 1970s was combined with high unemployment—a condition called stagflation.

Just as stagflation was hitting the hardest, the linking of Social Security benefits to the Consumer Price Index went into effect in 1975. A great increase in benefit costs resulted, far greater than had been expected, for when the plan was passed in 1972, no one had foreseen the high inflation combined with the high unemployment that took place in the 1970s.

Robert Myers, then chief actuary for the Social Security Administration, had testified on the formula for indexing benefits to cost of living in 1969, three years before its passage. He said the proposed formula "would very conservatively finance automatic benefit increases, unless we come to a time when there was a runaway inflation." However, Myers predicted confidently, " . . . that possibility can be ignored."

CHANGES IN THE POPULATION
AFFECT THE SYSTEM

There were other powerful forces at work creating pressure on the Social Security system. One of these was a long-term increase in the number of elderly in the population. In 1935, the average life expectancy at birth of an American was 61.7 years. In 1975, it was 72.5. By 1981, both in absolute numbers and in their proportion of the population, there were more elderly Americans than ever before.

The age of sixty-five for Social Security eligibility was set purposely low in 1935 because the planners wanted to make it possible for older workers to retire, thus creating more jobs for younger workers. By 1975, however, the greater number of Americans retiring at age sixty-five was putting a strain on the Social Security system's ability to pay.

In fact, more Americans were taking advantage of the option now offered to begin collecting benefits from ages sixty-two to sixty-four. There was a penalty for doing this; the recipient could collect, at age sixty-two, only 80 percent of the monthly benefits that would be paid if he or she waited until age sixty-five to begin collecting. Even though the reduced benefit would remain in force after the beneficiary passed sixty-five, about two-thirds of old-age beneficiaries in 1981 had chosen the early retirement option. This created a double squeeze. An early retiree was (1) not paying taxes to the system, and (2) was collecting benefits instead.

There was a demographic revolution occurring at the other end of the age scale as well. After World War II, the country experienced a "baby boom." Very large numbers of children had been born in relation to the total population. During the 1970s, the opposite was true. The birth rate fell to the lowest level in the country's history and showed no signs of increasing to its former level.

This baby boom-and-bust created an enormous long-term problem for the system. As those baby-boom children born between 1945 and 1960 reach retirement age in the twenty-first century, they will have to be supported by a much smaller number of working citizens. Right now there are more than three payroll taxpayers for each beneficiary. By the year 2020, the ratio is expected to fall to two to one. By that time, some estimates are that 53 million Americans will be living in retirement. To be ready for these retirees, changes must be made in the system, either by raising taxes drastically or by reducing benefits.

Ironically, the rise in the number of retirees that creates the problem also creates a large group of active citizens ready to oppose any reduction in benefits. A higher percentage of older people vote than any other age group. Also, the elderly are concentrated in key areas of the country. Forty-five percent of senior citizens live in seven states: California, New York, Florida, Illinois, Ohio, Pennsylvania, and Texas. Their votes are crucial in electing or defeating a candidate, even a presidential candidate.

In addition, the retired status of senior citizens enables them to use more of their time to lobby for issues of concern to them. The most important issue to them is Social Security. Few

Senior citizens, mostly retired, are an active political force. Here a senior-citizens' group known as the Gray Panthers has gathered to greet Senator Frank Church (D., Idaho) on his arrival in Portland, Oregon, in 1976.

politicians will risk the wrath of the "elderly lobby" by suggesting that benefits be lowered.

To discuss the political influence of the elderly is not to say that they are a favored part of our population. The 1980 census showed that 15.7 percent of all Americans over age sixty-five were living below the poverty level. This meant, in 1981, an income under $5,700 for a household of two persons.

Even so, these figures are an improvement on the past. In 1959, more than 35.2 percent of the elderly were estimated as living below the poverty level. The main reason why this figure has been cut in half is the rise in Social Security benefits.

A majority of the elderly today rely on Social Security for their survival. Their savings and private pension plans have not proved inflation-proof. Today, about half of American workers are protected by a private pension plan. Of those, only half—one in five retirees—fulfill the terms of the pension and receive full benefits. Workers who changed jobs in the past frequently lost their rights to the pension they earned in their former job. (In 1974, Congress passed a pension act that made it easier for workers to carry pension rights with them if they changed jobs; the effect of this act has still to be felt on large numbers of retirees.)

In addition, private pension plans do not ordinarily include health and disability provisions, as Social Security provides; nor do private plans generally include cost-of-living rises.

MATURITY OF THE SYSTEM
EXPOSES WEAKNESSES

The decade of the 1970s saw the maturing of the Social Security system, and its real costs became evident. It was no longer possible, as had been done in the early 1950s, to add more large groups to the system and increase the number of paying workers. The costs of added old-age, disability, and Medicare benefits became greater as greater numbers of people became eligible to receive them. The ratio of those who were paying in to those who were drawing out of the system assumed the proportion that would have to be permanently dealt with. In 1945, nearly forty-two workers paid into the system for each beneficiary. In 1950, the proportion of active workers to recipients was sixteen to one; when the program matured, it stabilized at around three to one—at least, until the twenty-first century.

It could now be seen that those who entered the system early received a good return for their payments. A worker who entered the system in 1937 and paid the maximum tax for thirty years would have paid a total of only $2,673.60 if he or she retired at the end of 1966. The worker would then receive a cash benefit of $218 a month. Thus, in little more than a year, he or she would receive all of what had been paid, and would continue to collect for life. A sixty-five-year-old or older nonworking spouse of a recipient would collect half of the working spouse's benefit. In case of the recipient's death, children under age twenty-two (today the age limit is nineteen) who were still in school could collect as well. (Of course, a direct comparison of money paid in to money collected is unfair; 1937 dollars were worth far more than 1967 dollars.)

On the other hand, a worker entering the system in 1968 will have paid $27,511.24 after only twenty years—provided that no further tax increases are passed during that time. That worker is supporting retirees with greater benefits, and greater numbers of retirees, than ever before.

Those who opposed the system were fond of citing outrageous examples of beneficiaries who received far more than they paid. A woman named Ida Fuller was among the first group of beneficiaries; she received her first benefit check in January 1940. By the time she died in a nursing home thirty-five years later at the age of 100, she had received more than $20,000 worth of benefits. All this for a total contribution of only $22 before her retirement. (Of course, this could happen in a private insurance plan as well.)

If there were any good effects of the disastrous economy of

the 1970s, it was in showing the true costs of the Social Security system and highlighting the problems of the future. Only by looking at these new realities can the Social Security system be saved for future retirees and future generations.

CHANGES IN THE CARTER YEARS

When Jimmy Carter was elected president in 1976, the Ford administration was already considering proposals for changing the Social Security system to bring costs in line with payments. Action on these proposals was left to the new administration.

The major problem was that as of 1975 benefits had been tied to the Consumer Price Index—which reflected prices. Tying benefits to prices had been expected to produce smaller increases than tying them to wages, which historically had risen faster than prices.

As with so many other things in the 1970s, the unexpected happened. Prices rose higher than wages. The effect can be seen in what happened to the replacement rate. The replacement rate shows what part of a worker's income will be paid by current Social Security benefits when he or she retires. In 1975, the replacement rate rose to about 67 percent for a married worker earning average wages and 92 percent for a married worker earning the minimum wage. These rates compared with 50 percent and 67 percent only ten years earlier.

In practical terms, the rise in replacement rates can be seen by the fact that in 1968 the average old-age payment was under $100 a month, but by 1977 the average was $240 a month, and for a retired couple, $400.

In the fall of 1977, Congress acted to stabilize the replacement rates in the first year of benefits at around 54 percent for a low-income worker, 42 percent for an average-income worker, and 26 percent for a high-income worker. These rates applied only to the primary benefit (the first year's payment). Current and future beneficiaries would continue to see a rise in their benefits tied to the Consumer Price Index.

There were other proposals in 1977 to change the system. Republican members of the House Ways and Means Committee proposed to gradually raise the age of eligibility for old-age benefits to compensate for the higher life expectancy of Americans. Supporters of this plan also argued that society should not discourage the elderly from working—by paying them to retire—because they could still be a productive part of society.

Even though current beneficiaries were not to be affected, the "elderly lobby" rose in opposition to the plan. The political pressure caused the proposal to be dropped. Independent party candidate John Anderson was to raise it again during the presidential election campaign of 1980.

President Carter also submitted a number of proposals to Congress that would have found new sources of revenue to cure the ills of the system. Carter proposed to tax employers on *all* wages and salaries paid, rather than limiting them to the maximum wage base that applied to workers. In addition, his administration proposed to use general revenues to pay benefits whenever the unemployment rate exceeded 6 percent. These revenues would supply whatever "lost" taxes would have been paid by the workers who were now unemployed. The proposal would be retroactive to 1975.

Adoption of the Carter proposals would have done away with the need for increasing the payroll tax, at least until 1985. But Congress rejected them. The Carter proposals violated two long-standing principles of the Social Security system: that the payroll tax was to be shared equally by employer and employee; and that general revenues were not to be a part of the retirement system.

Instead, the Democratic leadership in Congress proposed and passed its own bill, which Carter signed.

The final bill increased dramatically the maximum wage base on which the payroll tax was paid. This amount was to go to $22,900 in 1979, to $25,900 in 1980, and to $29,700 in 1981. From that point, the maximum wage base was to be raised auto-

matically in relation to increases in average wages. This contrasted with the limit of $3,000 for the original act and was a sizable leap from the wage base of $17,700 for 1978.

Congress also acted to liberalize the retirement test. A beneficiary aged sixty-five or over could continue to collect full benefits while earning more than the $4,000 permitted in 1978. The limit was to go in stages to $6,000 in 1982, and rise after that in connection with the average national wage. The retirement test was not relaxed for those under age sixty-five.

The 1977 amendments were hailed as the cure for the Social Security system. Experts predicted that the changes would protect the system at least until the 1990s. Once again, the experts were proved wrong by the workings of the economy. The Carter administration failed to solve the problems of inflation and unemployment, and Social Security was still locked into rises in the Consumer Price Index.

In 1979, President Carter proposed $600 million in Social Security cuts for the fiscal 1980 budget, a cut of less than 0.5 percent. But his political power was less than it had been, and Congress showed no inclination to cut the system in an election year. The proposal was defeated. Carter himself lost the 1980 election overwhelmingly to Ronald Reagan. Reagan entered office as a popular president with a mandate for change. Many wondered how he would handle the problems of the Social Security system.

4

REAGAN'S ATTEMPTS TO CHANGE THE SYSTEM

In the presidential campaign of 1980, Ronald Reagan pledged that his administration would remove the earnings restrictions on people receiving Social Security benefits. He also promised to preserve the cost-of-living increases that had gone into effect in the 1970s.

In contrast, Reagan's opposition to excessive government spending was well known. He promised to cut waste and inefficiency in government but gave no hint of the broad programs he would propose to accomplish this task.

His election, by an overwhelming majority in the electoral college, seemed to give him a mandate for change. Polls showed that the new president was popular with the majority of the American people. They seemed to be willing to give him a chance to make new kinds of programs work.

Given this background, it seemed that Reagan would have a good chance of making whatever reforms he thought necessary in the Social Security system. There was by 1981 general agreement that something had to be done to refinance the system, either by raising taxes or by reducing benefits, or some combination of the two. Projections brought the bankruptcy of the system uncomfortably close. Some said that sometime in 1982 or 1983 there would no longer be money in the trust funds to pay the benefits that Congress had approved. Was it possible that a month was approaching when some of the system's 36 million recipients would expect a check in their mailbox and find none?

In the first year of his administration Reagan would in fact introduce a program to change the Social Security system. The fate of his proposals provides a useful lesson in understanding why the system is so resistant to change.

THE SAFETY NET

Reagan promised the nation that his administration would produce a balanced federal budget by 1984. On February 18, 1981, not quite a month after taking office, the president appeared before Congress to present the budget proposals for his first year in office. There were many cuts in social programs, but the president asserted that " . . . all those with true need can rest assured that the social safety net of programs they depend on are exempt from any cuts."

As further details of his budget were released, it became clear that Reagan's "safety net" of protected programs included Social Security retirement and survivors' benefits and the Medicare program. These, the two most costly of the "safety net" programs, had no means test for recipients. Ironically, Medicaid, which provided services similar to the Medicare program, did have a means test; it was designed for the poor, and Reagan's budget cut its funding.

Reagan's reluctance to touch Social Security and Medicare seemed to confirm the belief of the programs' planners that only by keeping the programs free from a means test could they be protected from cuts in the future. The very fact that there were large numbers of people who received benefits under these programs seemed to protect them from Reagan's budget ax.

CONGRESS CONSIDERS
SOCIAL SECURITY

Despite Social Security's immunity from the early Republican budget cuts, the system still faced an uncertain future. In a reversal of form, Democrats led the way in proposing cuts and other changes in the system. On March 25, 1981, Representative J. J. Pickle of Texas, chairman of the House Social Security Subcommittee, made public the most promising proposals that he had reviewed. Among these were:

- Using general revenues to supply half the funds needed for HI (Part A Medicare). The Social Security taxes saved by this would be used to support the OASI fund.
- Raising the normal retirement age from sixty-five to sixty-eight in gradual stages from the years 2000 to 2012.
- Eliminating the earnings limitation for persons sixty-five and over.
- Tying the annual automatic increases in benefits to wages rather than prices.
- Changing the date of the annual automatic increase in benefits from July 3 to October 3.
- Phasing out the benefits for beneficiaries' children who were still attending school.
- Eliminating for future beneficiaries the minimum benefit of $122 a month that was paid to those who had spent only a short time contributing to the system.
- Placing a maximum total on the amount of money that can be received in disability benefits from public programs.

The most controversial of Pickle's proposals were using general funds for HI and changing the basis of the indexing of benefits. The president let it be known that he was opposed to both proposals. Republican Representative Bill Gradison said that using general revenues would create "a tragic precedent" by moving the program toward a welfare status and away from a right earned by contributors. This was the same argument used by the system's planners during the Roosevelt administration.

Experts testified that adopting Pickle's proposal to support HI with general funds would cost the government $20 billion a year. That would require a 5.7 percent increase in personal income taxes, something the president unalterably opposed.

Robert Myers, deputy commissioner of the Social Security Administration, told Pickle's House subcommittee that the Reagan administration was in the process of deciding whether to cut benefits or increase payroll taxes, or a combination, to meet the deficit in Social Security funds.

Pickle responded to Myers that the need for action was urgent. He said that beginning in 1984 the Social Security fund would not have enough assets to cover benefits.

As for the proposal to change the indexing system of benefits, once Reagan let his opposition be known, there was no chance of its being adopted. Democratic Representative Richard A. Gephardt said the proposal was "too much political dynamite for anyone to walk the plank with." If it were to pass, both the administration and congressional Democrats "should walk it together."

Even so, in a vote on March 31, 1981, the House subcommittee on Social Security approved shifting the cost-of-living increase from July to October, placing a cap on disability benefits received from all programs (equal to 80 percent of a person's former earnings), and rounding down the monthly benefit checks to the nearest dollar. This last change alone was estimated as producing a savings of $500 million by 1986, so large had the program become.

On May 7, the same subcommittee approved some major changes in the system:

• The age at which a person can retire with full benefits was to rise from sixty-five to sixty-eight, phased in over ten years beginning in 1990. That would eventually mean lower benefits for four out of every five Social Security recipients.

• The earnings limitation for all beneficiaries would be eliminated at age sixty-eight rather than the current seventy-two.

• Those choosing the option to retire at age sixty-two would have their benefits permanently reduced by 36 percent rather than the current 20 percent.

The net effect of the last two proposals would be to encourage people to continue working longer, and thus pay payroll taxes for a longer time than they normally would have.

The subcommittee's recommendations were a significant change in the way Congress dealt with Social Security. But passage by the subcommittee was a long way from passage by the full House and Senate and approval by the president. Nonetheless, the subcommittee's bold action put pressure on the Senate and the White House to respond to the need for changes in the system.

On May 8, 1981, the Senate approved a proposal that would delay the payment of increases from July to October. The Senate also approved basing the yearly benefit increase either on the Consumer Price Index or on the average increase in wages, whichever was *lower*. The House still had not acted on its subcommittee's proposals.

THE REAGAN
ADMINISTRATION'S PLAN

On May 12, 1981, Reagan's secretary for Health and Human Services, Richard Schweiker, announced the administration's plan for changing the Social Security system:

• Beginning in January 1987, the formula for figuring a worker's primary benefit (the base monthly payment that would rise annually) would be changed. Workers with average wages retiring on or after that time would receive about 4 percent less; workers with higher wages would receive about 9 percent less. The average replacement rate would be around 38 percent. This step would produce the greatest savings of the president's proposals.

• Those who turned sixty-two after January 1982 would receive a sharp cut in benefits if they chose the option to retire early. Reagan proposed to reduce the early-retirement benefits by a maximum of 45 percent instead of the current 20 percent. This was a steeper cut than the 36 percent proposed by the House subcommittee. On the average, it would mean an early retiree's monthly check would be $126 less than under current law.

• The annual rise in benefits would be delayed from July to October, as in the House subcommittee's proposal. However, the president fulfilled an earlier pledge to keep the annual rise tied to the Consumer Price Index, and not to the rise in wages.

• Federal and some state employees are not covered by the Social Security program. However, some of them work in covered jobs before or after their government service. In the past, it has been possible for these employees to collect both a government pension and sizable Social Security benefits. The administration proposed to take the government pension into account when calculating Social Security benefits for these people, thus lowering their benefits.

• Sick pay for workers is not now subject to Social Security taxes. The president proposed to tax sick pay for the first six months a worker received it.

• In 1981, the "retirement test," or the ceiling on the amount a beneficiary aged sixty-five or over could earn while still collecting full benefits, was $5,500 a year. The president proposed to raise this maximum to $10,000 in 1983, $15,000 in 1984, $20,000 in 1985, and eliminate it entirely after that. This went farther than the House subcommittee's proposal.

• The administration proposed to tighten the requirements for a worker applying for Social Security disability payments. Workers must prove they would be disabled for twenty-four months, instead of the current twelve. They would have to wait six months, instead of five, to begin collecting benefits. Disability would be judged on medical conditions only, without taking into account whether age, education, and work experience would keep the worker from finding a new job under his or her disability—as was the case with the current program. Also, to be eligible for disability payments, a worker would have to have paid Social Security taxes for thirty of the last forty calendar quarters, instead of the current rule of twenty out of forty.

• Congress had passed in 1977 a schedule of rising taxes to pay for Social Security. The tax was to increase gradually until it reached 7.65 percent in 1990. The Reagan administration proposed to lower the tax rate whenever the money in Social Security trust funds reached 50 percent of the amount that would have to be paid in the following year.

Secretary Schweiker was optimistic about the effect that the administration's proposals would have and said that if they were enacted, "We will be able to reduce the Social Security tax rate increase now scheduled for 1985 and to actually decrease Social Security tax rates by 1990 below what they are today." He said this would mean that a young worker entering the labor force in 1982 would save an average of $33,600 in Social Security taxes during her or his lifetime. The Reagan administration disregarded entirely the House subcommittee's proposal to raise the age at which workers could qualify for benefits. Adoption of the administration program was estimated to provide an immediate savings of $9 billion in fiscal 1982 and an annual savings of $24 billion by 1986.

REACTION TO
THE REAGAN PLAN

The Democratic leadership of Congress had been stung by the ease with which President Reagan had pushed his earlier budget cuts through Congress. They saw Social Security as a key issue on which to oppose the president.

The Democratic Speaker of the House, Representative Thomas P. (Tip) O'Neill, Jr., led the attack. He said, "I will be fighting [the president's program] every inch of the way, and I hope that will be the position of every member of my party." His remarks that the president's proposal was "despicable," "a breach of faith," and "a rotten thing to do" were widely quoted. Other Democrats joined in O'Neill's condemnation.

Some kept cooler heads. Representative Pickle urged Congress "to reserve our gunpowder" until the administration had submitted to detailed questioning on the proposals before his subcommittee and other congressional bodies. Democratic Representative Thomas Foley, the House majority whip, called for "a bipartisan consensus on Social Security." He said, "We have to defuse this highly charged political issue."

The president's proposals clearly demanded an extensive rethinking of the issue, and in the joint House-Senate conference that met to work out a uniform budget proposal, the earlier changes passed by the Senate were thrown out. While the president's proposals were being considered, Congress would refrain from any action.

Meanwhile, many groups in the Social Security lobby were organizing opposition to the president's plan. Wilbur J. Cohen, head of the Save Our Security coalition, said that Reagan's proposal would have "disruptive consequences equal to Watergate in its impact on individuals' attitude toward government." It would "destroy people's confidence in the institution of Social Security."

The president of the National Council on the Aging said that "the president's safety net is under water, and old people are being thrown to the sharks." The president of the National Council of Senior Citizens said the president's plan was "the biggest frontal attack on Social Security ever launched—an attack aimed at the ultimate destruction of the system."

These statements might have been extreme, but they seemed to represent the sentiments of a majority of Americans. A *Washington Post*-ABC News poll announced four days after the plan was released showed that Americans disapproved of the Reagan Social Security proposals by a margin of 3 to 2. Furthermore, among those who had formed an opinion, two out of every three thought that they would be hurt rather than helped by the president's plan.

Public reaction was strong enough to make Republicans nervous. The party's Tidewater Conference attributed the problems in the Social Security system to "abysmal neglect of past Democratic-dominated Congresses," and challenged the Democrats to come up with something better than the president's proposals. Even so, the conference stopped short of endorsing the president's plan.

The week after he announced the proposals, Secretary Schweiker said Reagan was willing to compromise. "We would certainly strongly consider working out a bipartisan bill," Schweiker told panelists on a radio news program. Republican Senator Robert Dole, chairman of the Senate Finance Committee, said the president's proposals would face "a lot of compromises."

THE REAGAN PLAN—
PROS AND CONS

The most controversial of President Reagan's proposals was the plan to reduce by 45 percent the benefits of those who chose early retirement. On the face of it, the proposal seemed justified by the fact that fully 70 percent of all current retirees took the option of retiring early, even with a loss of up to 20 percent of their benefits. Reducing the number of early retirees by making the penalty harsher would keep more workers on the job, contributing to the economy and paying the payroll tax.

The president's opponents argued that those who chose early retirement were not doing so simply because they found retirement an appealing choice. A 1976 Social Security Administration report showed that 54 percent of the workers who retired at sixty-two were in poor health. Another 20 percent had lost their jobs or were forced to retire. Only 17 percent actually had the clear option of retiring or continuing in their current jobs.

Furthermore, the president's plan would have put this provision into effect almost immediately—by the following January. This appeared cruel to those who would have expected to retire early the following year. The speed with which the penalty would take effect went against all previous proposals to drastically change the system, in that it did not allow enough time for future retirees to plan a retirement schedule.

Another controversial feature of Reagan's plan was to drastically raise, and eventually eliminate, the amount a beneficiary could earn without lowering his or her benefits. This fulfilled Reagan's campaign pledge, but to many it seemed that Reagan was rewarding those who were well off by enabling them to continue working and collect benefits at the same time.

In fact, the retirement test had been controversial for several years. Though it provided a test on earned income from a job, it did not take into account what the government called "unearned income," which included stock dividends, interest payments, rent on property, royalties, and many other kinds of income. Someone holding a job paying only $6,000 a year in 1981 would face a loss in benefits of $250 a year and would have to pay payroll taxes on his or her $6,000 income as well. But a retiree who had no job could collect any amount in rents, dividends, or interest without losing a penny in Social Security benefits. Those who supported the elimination of the retirement test claimed that it was the poorer beneficiaries who suffered most from it.

There were other objections to Reagan's proposals. They would not affect the benefits of anyone currently collecting. Though this was the wisest political course—because those retirees constituted a formidable political pressure group, and many of them had voted for Reagan—some claimed it was unfair. By their reasoning, if the system was too costly, everyone should share the burden of changing it. In fact, this argument went, those currently collecting had paid less in payroll taxes than the generation of workers who would be hurt by Reagan's plan. Government statistics showed that a married worker retiring at age sixty-five in 1979 could expect to receive four and a half times what he or she had paid into the system, *even with inflation taken into account.* The system's beneficiaries in 1981 were receiving a better return on their money than any future beneficiaries could expect to get. Why shouldn't they accept a small decrease to keep the system solvent for the future retirees?

Other aspects of the Reagan plan will be discussed in Chapter Five.

CONGRESS ACTS ON SOCIAL SECURITY

On May 20, 1981, only eight days after the announcement of Reagan's plan, the Senate handed the president a stunning defeat. It passed a resolution, by a vote of 96–0, rejecting two of the cuts he had sought. The Senate resolution said, "Congress shall not precipitously and unfairly penalize early retirees," and "will not support reductions in benefits which exceed those necessary to achieve a financially sound system." The latter part of the resolution was a reaction to a report released the day before by the House Select Committee on Aging. The report said that the Reagan cuts would save more than twice the amount needed to keep the system solvent over the next seventy-five years.

The day after the Senate resolution, Reagan indicated his willingness to compromise. He said he had instructed Secretary Schweiker to meet with congressional leaders "to launch a bipartisan effort to save Social Security." The president said he would insist on only three main principles in a Social Security plan: (1) he opposed the use of general revenues to support the system and any changes in the basic benefit structure; (2) he wanted to hold down payroll taxes to support the system; and (3) he wanted to eliminate all abuses "that can rob the elderly of their rightful legacy."

In June, the major budget bill for the government passed both houses of Congress. In it were certain changes relating to Social Security that were estimated to provide a savings of $2.7 billion. Most of the cuts were technical revisions, such as the plan to round down monthly payments to the nearest dollar. One of the approved cuts would explode into another controversy, however. Congress voted to eliminate the current $122 minimum monthly benefit for all retirees, including those currently receiving benefits.

Though the administration endorsed the proposal, it went further than Reagan's original plan (which contained no cuts for current beneficiaries) except in delaying the annual date of raising benefits.

Both houses of Congress had approved substantially the same cuts in Social Security. But the overall budget for the government had certain differences that had to be ironed out in a joint committee of Congress. As the committee continued to deliberate, opposition rose against any cuts in Social Security.

Some Democrats sought to gain politically from the modest Social Security cuts that Congress had approved. Democratic Senator Daniel P. Moynihan said Republicans were conducting "a campaign of political terrorism." He added, "By cutting benefits we would be taking money away from the household budgets of millions of Americans and putting it into the president's budget to make it look better." (Even though the three funds of the Social Security system are separate from the federal budget, for accounting purposes a surplus in them offsets any deficit in the federal budget overall. Changes in Social Security are considered along with ordinary federal budget requests.)

The $122 minimum benefit became a rallying point for those who wanted to keep Social Security as it was. Democrats on the House Committee on Aging said that removing the minimum benefit would actually *cost* the government around $2 billion over five years, because the beneficiaries who lost Social Security payments would have to go on welfare and Medicaid.

Those who wanted to appeal to the Social Security lobby seized on the issue of the $122 minimum benefit. It was easy to understand, and the issue seemed to be one of defending the poor who collected only a minimum benefit against those who wanted to gut the system.

In fact, the elimination of the minimum benefit was a way of reducing the benefits of those who were collecting other pensions, such as federal and state workers who had a separate pension plan but often had worked for a short time in Social Security–covered jobs. Unfortunately, the elimination of the benefit would have hurt others who might really have needed it.

Robert Myers, deputy Social Security commissioner, told a House subcommittee that of the three million retirees now receiving the minimum pension, all but 140,000 would keep the benefit, be able to supplement it with welfare payments, or have additional income from a federal or state pension or from a working spouse.

But the issue had become too hot. By the end of the legislative session, both the House and Senate had agreed to restore the $122 minimum benefit for most recipients.

Even so, in July, the House-Senate joint committee agreed on some savings in Social Security by: (1) tightening standards for Medicare and disability payments; (2) delaying payment of early retirement benefits until the month after the retiree's sixty-second birthday; (3) cutting off benefits for college students aged eighteen to twenty-two whose parents were beneficiaries; and (4) making certain other technical changes.

REAGAN'S RESPONSE
Faced with the nearly complete defeat of his proposals, President Reagan scheduled a nationally televised speech on the sub-

ject of Social Security. Republicans urged him to change his mind. A poll taken for the Republican Congressional Campaign Committee showed that 66 percent of Americans were opposed to any change in Social Security benefits. Another poll indicated that if the system had to be changed to keep it going, two out of three Americans preferred raising the payroll tax to cutting benefits.

When the president finally delivered his speech, on July 27, 1981, he spoke on general economic issues. His major proposal concerning Social Security was the establishment of a bipartisan panel, with members selected by the White House and leaders of the House and Senate. The committee would be composed of seven Democrats, seven Republicans, and one independent. The panel would discuss and recommend ways to avoid the imminent shortfall in Social Security funds.

Later in the year, advisers to the president said he would propose no new changes in Social Security in 1982—an election year. The bipartisan panel's report was not expected to be delivered until sometime in 1983.

LESSONS OF THE
REAGAN PROPOSALS

The fate of Reagan's plan to change Social Security showed the great support the program had. Intense opposition doomed Reagan's proposed changes almost from the start. More than ninety groups, including unions, senior citizens, teachers, and others, united in opposition to his plan. Their membership was estimated at 40 million adult Americans. Many more people wrote members of Congress and the White House or otherwise expressed their disapproval of change in Social Security.

A first-year president, with the electoral majority that Reagan had, is supposed to be at the height of his influence. Reagan's power showed itself in the ease with which his other programs, some of them quite radical and far-reaching in their effects, sailed through Congress. Social Security was virtually the only major issue on which Reagan was defeated in his first year in office.

Yet both short-term and long-term deficits in the system seemed clearly to threaten it. Change was needed. The report of the bipartisan committee might help sway a majority behind those changes.

5

THE FUTURE OF SOCIAL SECURITY

Despite President Reagan's first-year failure to persuade Congress to accept meaningful cuts in the Social Security program, there was widespread agreement that the program was in danger of running out of funds. Estimates differed as to the date bankruptcy would occur, and also as to the precise amount of shortfall over the short term. Estimates of the deficit over the five years following 1981 ranged from $11 billion to $111 billion.

It was impossible to make a precise estimate because much depended on the state of the economy. If wages failed to rise as steeply as prices, then the payroll tax payments coming into the system would again fail to keep up with the benefits, which were still tied to prices. Inflation in the 1980s was as difficult to predict as it had been in the 1970s. There was also the problem of rising unemployment. The more people out of work, the fewer people there would be contributing to the system through the payroll tax. In fairness, it should be mentioned that two recognized experts on the system disputed the deficit figures and the need for change. Robert Ball, long-time Social Security commissioner who had urged many of the benefit rises in the early

1970s, and Wilbur Cohen, secretary of Health, Education, and Welfare in the Johnson administration, said that the deficit figures were too high. They said the predictions of bankruptcy for the Social Security system were based on a pessimistic view of developments in the national economy.

Reagan's advisors admitted that the president's initial plan on Social Security had erred on the side of safety. The planners anticipated that some cuts would be reduced by Congress, and they wanted to prepare the system for the worst-case economic conditions. If there were, in fact, better economic times in the 1980s, and the Social Security system developed a surplus, well and good, Reagan supporters argued. Unlike their counterparts in the 1930s, Republican leaders now had no objections to building up a large reserve fund, because the long-range difficulties in the system were as inevitable as the short-range problems. And "hard" statistics for the long-range period were easier to come by.

The 1980 census showed that the number of people aged sixty-five and older grew 20 percent in the 1970–1980 decade. In 1980, this group numbered 25.5 million, or 11.3 percent of the total population. By the year 2020, the number of people in this age group would swell to 53 million because of the post–World War II baby boom.

The median age of the American population was only twenty-three in 1900. By 1950, it had peaked at age thirty. The baby boom caused a twenty-year decline, to age twenty-eight in 1970. But the trend reversed quickly because of the low birth rates in the 1970s, and by 1980, the median was again thirty. With life-expectancy rates rising, that figure would continue to rise.

As we have seen, demographic predictions showed that it would eventually require the taxes of two Americans to support the benefits of one beneficiary, a ratio significantly harder to bear than the present 3.2 to 1. The sooner changes are made in the Social Security system to correct this long-term imbalance, the easier they will be—both on workers (if the solution involves higher taxes) and on retirees (if the solution involves lower benefits). Congress's unwillingness to act in 1981 did not augur well for the prospect of change.

TEMPORARY CHANGES
FOR THE SHORT RUN

The political cost of letting Social Security run out of funds is probably too great for Congress to allow it to happen, at least in the short run. There are at least two ways of changing the system that Congress could adopt to meet temporary shortfalls:

1. Transfers between the funds. The original fund set up to administer Social Security retirement funds is now known as the Old Age and Survivors Insurance (OASI) fund. There are two additional payroll tax-supported funds, for hospital insurance (HI) and disability insurance (DI). Congress sets a formula dividing the payroll tax money among these three funds. At present, benefits for each of the three main parts can be paid only from the fund earmarked for it.

In the five years from 1982 to 1986, both the DI and HI funds were expected to show a surplus. If the OASI fund were allowed to borrow from this surplus, it could stay solvent at least until 1988, according to Congressional Budget Office Director Alice M. Rivlin, testifying before a committee in 1981. (Rivlin pointed out that bad economic conditions could cause insolvency as early as 1984, even if fund-borrowing were allowed.) The Senate Democratic Caucus subsequently endorsed the fund-borrowing solution, but no action was taken by the full Congress.

This solution, though only a short-term one, seemed likely to eventually win congressional approval, for it offered a longer period of solvency without the need for raising taxes or cutting benefits. The chief objection was that it only postponed the need for doing something more substantial to change the system—one more example of "hiding the costs" of the system so that a later Congress would have to deal with it.

Furthermore, the prediction that the system could be "saved" until 1988 by interfund borrowing was based on good economic conditions in the period. A second report, from the actuaries of the Social Security system, presented to the House Ways and Means Committee in 1981, showed that Medicare costs took an unexpectedly high jump in 1981. The HI fund might have less money available than the earlier report showed. It was possible that the three funds combined would fall below "safe" levels by 1984 or 1985.

2. Using general revenues for benefits. Whenever the Social Security system has appeared shaky, one of the suggestions offered has usually been to support it with general revenues— the government funds collected by personal income tax, business taxes, excise taxes, and the other sources of federal income. This suggestion was again raised in 1981.

The original reason for rejecting general funding still seemed sound to many—that it would weaken the idea of Social Security as a right earned by those who had paid into it. It would appear unfair to take the taxes of those citizens who were not members to pay benefits they would never collect. It would make Social Security more of a "welfare" program.

The Reagan administration came out solidly against this proposal, because it would interfere with the general economic plan that Reagan and his advisors envisioned. Use of general revenues would worsen the federal budget deficit, which Reagan hoped to reduce or eliminate. Use of general revenues might require a rise in general taxes. Reagan had already pushed a three-year tax cut through Congress and resisted attempts to revoke any part of it, for he hoped this would stimulate the economy.

Nevertheless, if all other attempts to reform Social Security failed, it seemed Congress might approve use of general revenues instead of cutting benefits in a sizable way.

CHANGES WITHIN THE SYSTEM

There were certain technical changes that Congress could authorize in the Social Security system to improve both short-term and long-term finances. Almost all of these would cause some pain, either among tax-paying workers or benefit-collecting retirees. But they would probably all at least be seriously considered by the bipartisan committee that President Reagan appointed to recommend changes in the system. None of them would be a sharp break with the past goals and methods of Social Security.

Raising the minimum age. Clearly the easiest way of cutting benefits in Social Security would be to raise the minimum age required for eligibility. To ease the blow, this could be done gradually and on a long-term basis so that people could plan for it. A commission authorized by Congress in 1977 recommended raising the age from sixty-five to sixty-eight in gradual stages beginning in the year 2000 and ending in the year 2012. As we have seen, in 1981 the House Social Security Subcommittee recommended a similar plan to take effect between 1990 and 2000.

To many this seemed a fair plan, designed to reflect the aging demographics of the population. Better health care not only enabled Americans to live longer, it enabled them to stay healthy longer and presumably able to continue working longer. Furthermore, because it would not cut the benefits of those currently collecting, it would be easier for Congress to accept.

Nevertheless, such a profound change could have unforeseen consequences. No one knew what the reaction would be of those now paying into the system.

Some planners have tried to estimate the effect such a change would have on private pension plans, offered to most union members and to many other workers by the companies that employ them. These pension plans commonly offer benefits at age sixty-five, as do private insurance plans purchased by those who anticipate retirement at that age. Some private companies offer "offset integrated" plans, which take Social Security benefits into account when calculating pension payments. Raising the age of eligibility for Social Security could put a financial strain on private pension plans, unless they also raised the normal retirement age. It could also disrupt the plans of workers who based their retirement security on the prospect of retiring at age sixty-five. Certainly any such change in raising the Social Security retirement age must be done on a long-range basis, to allow time for preparation.

Encouraging workers to continue in their jobs until age sixty-eight would also slow down the promotions of younger workers. It was not known whether older workers performed significantly better or worse than younger ones.

There was in addition the disquieting report that half of those who retire before age sixty-five today do so because of ill health or because they cannot find a job. Would these workers have to seek welfare payments or otherwise suffer if the retirement age were raised?

Changing the automatic increase in benefits. President Reagan's proposed change in applying the Consumer Price Index to the annual rise in benefits, by delaying it until October of each year, was only a stop-gap measure. Even so, it was so unpopular that Congress failed to pass it. Nonetheless, many saw the annual automatic raise as one of the chief problems of the system.

When the change was approved in 1972, it was thought that the application of an automatic change would take the responsibility for raising benefits out of the hands of Congress and thus remove political pressure from it. But the raises have proved to be unrealistically high.

It could be eliminated altogether, although that seemed only a slim possibility. Any Congress or president attempting to do so would face almost unbearable pressure from the beneficiaries. Yet there were many reasons for saying that the current system was unjustified. The Consumer Price Index includes such things as the cost of buying a house. Most retirees do not make that kind of purchase.

It is also argued that protecting retirees—or any other group—from the effects of inflation in a sense creates the climate in which inflation is possible. The incomes of those paying *into* the system are not generally protected against inflation. Protecting retirees creates a pressure group that lobbies for more inflationary benefits. Inflation is a national problem that will not be solved until the effects of it are felt by all segments of the population.

Furthermore, those who enjoyed the raises in benefits that the automatic increases brought were receiving far more than they had paid into the system. For them to argue that it was their "right" was not reasonable, in view of the contributions they had made and the strain these raises were putting on the system.

Congress could do several things to lower the annual automatic increase: (1) tie the increase to either wages or prices, whichever was lower; (2) make the rise based on less than 100 percent—75 or 80 percent—of consumer prices; or (3) put a ceiling on the rise, so that it would not increase benefits paid more than the rise in tax payments. Any of these plans would cause political trouble for a Congress that voted for them, but in the long term such changes might prove necessary.

Separating Medicare from the system. In 1981, a worker paid 6.65 percent of his or her wages, up to $29,700, for Social Security—4.7 percent to OASI, 0.65 percent to DI, and 1.3 percent to the HI fund. Though the HI fund was solvent, medical costs were rising at a rate higher than anyone had predicted. It was not as easy to predict or control what the costs of Medicare would be in the future as it was to predict the number of future retirees. In 1981, trustees of the fund—three Cabinet officers—

reported that the HI fund seemed likely to be exhausted in the early 1990s.

Some argued that because health insurance went so far beyond the original purpose of Social Security, the HI fund should be separated from the OASI and DI funds. Under this plan, HI would be paid for from general revenues, and the other two funds could be placed on a sound financial basis using the current rates of payroll taxation.

This would be a quick way to solve the problems of the old-age retirement fund, but it would endanger the HI program. Paid for out of general revenues, it would more closely resemble a national health insurance plan. Congress has always resisted setting up such a plan; it would be opposed by doctors' groups and others opposed to "socialized medicine."

A compromise plan, offered by Representative Pickle in 1981, would be to pay half of Medicare from general revenues and half from the payroll tax. Many of the labor unions and organizations of retirees who opposed the Reagan cuts indicated their willingness to accept Pickle's proposal. Their cooperation and support might mean that this would be one of the major changes in Social Security that Congress could adopt during the 1980s. Congress had found it acceptable to make certain cuts in the Medicare program during the budget debates of 1981, and Secretary Schweiker indicated that the administration would propose additional cuts in the future.

Including government employees in the plan. Full-time civilian federal employees, and some state and city employees, are not members of the Social Security plan. They have their own pension programs. As has been stated, some of them become "double-dippers"—they collect government pensions and Social Security retirement payments that were earned in private jobs either before, during, or after their government service. Their exemption has left a large number of people outside Social Security—the federal government is the largest single employer in the country.

Reagan's proposed 1981 Social Security cuts included refiguring the Social Security benefits given to former government employees. This was only a half-measure, compared to including them as full, paying members of the Social Security program.

Federal employees argued against this, pointing out that in 1981 they contributed 7 percent of their total salary (with no maximum) each year to their government pension fund—more than Social Security workers did. Moreover, the benefits from their pension fund are taxable; Social Security benefits are not. They argue that their overall contribution is greater than that of Social Security beneficiaries, even though the federal government contributes 33 percent of its employees' pension costs.

On the other hand, the total pension of federal and state workers (combined with their Social Security benefits, if they worked in private industry) is larger than if they were covered only by Social Security.

The struggle in 1981 to eliminate the minimum monthly benefit for Social Security was aimed mainly at those government workers who were "double-dippers." In an editorial of September 12, 1981, the *Washington Post* said of federal workers "their average lifetime earnings counted by Social Security are low, and the benefits they receive are very high compared with their contributions. Federal pensioners thus benefit unfairly—to the tune of almost $1 billion a year—from provisions in the Social Security law intended to help the poor . . ."

Raising the payroll tax. As has been noted, when Reagan's 1981 cuts were proposed, a majority of polled Americans said they preferred a higher Social Security tax to lowering of benefits. The question remained, how high a tax would be necessary?

The answer was, no one really knew. Current law projected

a payroll tax rise to 7.65 percent (for both worker and employer, a total of 15.3 percent) in 1990. The advisory commission set up by Congress in 1977 said that by the year 2025 the tax would reach 9 percent, which it recommended as the upper limit.

What, exactly, was the upper limit? People complained about Social Security taxes, as they did about all taxes, but the lesson of President Reagan's first year seemed to be that people did not want Social Security benefits cut, now or in the future.

The great fear was the turning point, sometime in the twenty-first century, when too few people would be paying too much in tax for too many beneficiaries. If that turning point was reached, and Congress had not done something to reduce benefits by some other method, then drastic changes in the system might be necessary.

BREAKS WITH THE PAST

Some proposals for changing the Social Security system would do more than merely adjust it. For example, the proposals to "bail out" a short-term shortfall in the system by the use of general revenues could develop into a long-term plan. Would it be wise to finance Social Security entirely by general revenues and make the payroll tax part of federal personal and business income tax?

Some people think such an action would be more honest than the current system. Peter Passell, an editor of the *New York Times*, wrote in 1981, "Social Security payroll taxes have never paid for more than a small fraction of the benefits promised. The system only muddles through by taxing today's workers to pay for today's retirees."

On the other hand, people at least know how much they are being taxed for Social Security under the current system. If the system has a deficit, the problem will be immediately apparent. Combine the system with the federal budget, and the deficit will be "concealed." John A. Svahn, head of the Social Security

Administration during the Reagan administration, said in an interview, "We don't want to go to general revenue, because once you eliminate the fiscal discipline of the trust fund and the dedicated tax, it becomes all too easy to finance the program out of the deficit, so to speak. Print more money. That fuels inflation, and inflation hits people who are retired and disabled much harder than it does other people."

Placing more emphasis on need. If the financial demands of a social security system like the one we have today become too great—on a long-term, permanent basis—the system could adjust by installing a "means test." Benefits would be paid only to those who met some criteria for need. These criteria could be generous, to pay as many people as possible, or they could be strict, to pay a greatly reduced number of people.

The retirement test already in effect is a kind of means test. Full Social Security benefits are only payable to persons aged sixty-five or over who have an income below $6,000. (This was for 1982; the amount was scheduled to rise thereafter with average wages.) When income rises above that level, benefits are reduced $2 for every $1 earned. Persons above the age of seventy-two (age seventy after 1982) have no maximum on earned income.

But this income limitation applies only to wages and salary earned in a job. Any recipient may have an unlimited amount of income from stock dividends, interest payments, private pensions, or other kinds of nonsalary income. The system creates what some see as an unfair bias; people who actually have a very high income (from nonsalary sources) can collect full benefits, while a worker without extra income sources can only earn a small amount before having his or her benefits reduced.

People argue that *all* types of income should be considered in deciding who should receive full benefits. The fairness of this seems obvious, until the consequences are considered. Those who own stocks, collect private pensions, or have interest-bearing accounts, usually saved during their preretirement years to get them. Private pensions generally require contributions from those who will someday collect them. Would it penalize these persons unfairly to reduce their Social Security benefits as a result? Would such a step actually discourage people from saving and providing for their retirement by private means?

President Reagan tried to go in the other direction and make the retirement test much more liberal, so that everyone above age sixty-five could collect full benefits, whatever their income.

The thorny problem of the retirement test has its roots in the original two-sided nature of the plan—welfare or insurance? As we have seen, it was neither fully welfare (which would pay benefits only to those who needed it) nor insurance (which would guarantee payments to everyone who paid in).

Robert Myers, deputy commissioner for Social Security under Reagan, stated the case for those who believe the plan ought to be more insurance than welfare: "The amounts paid in benefits are . . . based . . . on the contributions the person has paid into the system. It is not a needs-test program. A man with a billion dollars may not need Social Security, but he is just as much entitled as anyone else."

Yet the question persists: Does it serve society to have a man with a billion dollars collecting benefits he does not need from a social program?

Many would answer yes. Their reasoning is that if there were a real means test for collecting benefits, then the program would become "a program for the poor." Many people—not just those with a billion dollars—would resent paying into the system, for they would realize that they would never collect benefits. The consensus of opinion that has sustained Social Security would be broken. In hard economic times, when recipients needed the benefits most, the program would be cut, just as were the "welfare" types of social programs under the Reagan administration.

Taxing benefits. In November 1981, even a *rumor* that some members of the Budget Committee were thinking of proposing to tax Social Security benefits caused the Senate to pass, by 72 to 0, a resolution opposing such a move.

Of all the rights retirees believe they have earned by contributing to Social Security, one of the most cherished is the exemption of their benefits from taxation. There is something undeniably appealing about receiving a check every month and being able to say, "This is mine. The government cannot touch it."

Yet taxation of benefits is also one of the fairest ways suggested so far for making sure that Social Security benefits help those who need them most. It would be a kind of means test, for the percentage of tax paid would be tied to the progressive federal income tax. Those who had other income sources in their old age (dividends, interest, private pensions, etc.—all of which are already taxable) would pay a higher percentage than those who depended only, or mostly, on Social Security payments for their income.

All the arguments against a means test apply to taxing benefits as well. It is highly unlikely that Congress would in the near future approve such a proposal, unless it were linked to qualifying changes. The Committee for Economic Development, a nonpartisan study group, urged taxation of benefits along with abolishing the retirement test. Another possibility would be to tax only the benefits of those who have substantial outside income.

Making the system more like insurance. Any combination of the plans discussed in this chapter may be used to amend the Social Security program. One such comprehensive plan is the Equity Reform Plan of the National Federation of Independent Businesses. It would place the payroll tax payments of workers into an interest-bearing fund, like the one now established. At the time of a worker's retirement, the amount of money he or she personally accumulated would be totaled. Actuarial estimates would be made of the number of years the worker could expect to live. The accumulated funds would be paid in monthly installments on that basis. (The payments would continue for life; payments for those workers living longer than the actuarial estimate would be balanced by the excess funds of workers who lived a shorter time than the actuarial estimate.)

Under this plan, it can be seen that some workers will not have accumulated enough payments to ensure a decent standard of living. Their monthly benefits would be supplemented out of general revenues in a separate part of the program. Congress would set the level of income to be maintained by the second, supplementary, part of the program.

There are as many arguments in favor of and against this combination plan as there are against the separate elements of it. It does show how a comprehensive plan might work.

SOCIAL SECURITY, PRIVATE PLANS, AND YOUR FUTURE

Will young people beginning work today collect their Social Security payments in the twenty-first century? The answer is very likely yes, but with one harsh condition. Those paying into the system now will in all probability not receive as good a return on their money as the earlier participants in the system. The decline in population and the uncertainties of the economy will probably result in a smaller economic base from which those benefits can be drawn. Accepting that as a reality, young people still have a better chance than any earlier American generation of supplementing their Social Security retirement payments with money from private pension plans.

The importance of private pension plans has increased in recent years. These plans include pension plans offered by businesses, organized by unions, and sold by private insurance companies, as well as Individual Retirement Accounts (IRAs) set up by the beneficiary. As if in reaction to the strains on Social Security, Congress has passed legislation in recent years making it easier for workers to collect from these private plans and to set up their own IRAs.

Beginning in 1982, it was possible for *any* worker to set up his or her own IRA. Money paid into this account (which must be administered by a financial institution) was not to be taxed until the worker began to draw it out after retirement, when his or her tax rate would likely be lower. The maximum nontaxable contribution each year was set at $2,000 for a single person and $4,000 for a married couple.

The money put into IRAs can increase with interest over the years to produce a startling amount. Banks advertised that a worker putting the maximum $2,000 into an IRA beginning at age twenty-five, presuming an interest rate of 12 percent, would have a nest egg of $1,718,000 at age sixty-five. The figure would be double for a married couple contributing the maximum $4,000.

Remember, however, that no one knows what $1.7 million will buy forty years from now. If the interest rate is 12 percent, inflation may be equal to or above that level.

No one can predict what the impact of the liberalized pension laws will be. If they result in large numbers of people setting up their own pensions, there might be less of a need for high Social Security payments in the future. The millions of Americans who receive Social Security checks each month are a formidable force in keeping the system as it is, because they are literally fighting for their livelihood. If they had access to a private plan like those available today, their need might not be so great.

When Franklin Roosevelt signed the original Social Security Act in 1935, he said, "We can never insure 100 percent of the population against 100 percent of the hazards and vicissitudes of life, but we have tried to frame a law which will give some measure of protection to the average citizen and to his family . . . against poverty-ridden old age." The program succeeded beyond his expectations, largely because a majority of Americans trusted in the plan to provide for their own old age. If, as polls show, a majority of Americans no longer believe that, then it is time to consider some of the ways of repairing the covenant between generations that the program represents.

GLOSSARY

Benefits schedule—a method of calculating how much a recipient of Social Security may collect in monthly payments after retirement. The schedule is set by Congress and is based on the amount of wages a worker previously paid payroll tax on.

Consumer Price Index (CPI)—an average of selected prices that is intended to reflect the current cost of living, as compared to the indexes calculated in previous years.

Cost-of-living increase—see *indexing*.

DI—disability insurance. One of the three main funds of the Social Security program.

Double-dipper—a term applied to government employees who at retirement collect both from the federal pension plan and from Social Security because before, during, or after government service they also worked in private industry and paid payroll taxes into the Social Security program.

Dynamic earnings estimate—a basis for predicting the amount of money that the payroll tax will bring into the Social Security fund in future years. It is based on the premise that the economy will grow and that total wages will rise. Also called *dynamic earnings assumption.*

Earnings limitation—the maximum amount of wages that a worker can earn and still remain eligible for Social Security retirement benefits. Purpose is to show that a person has truly retired from full-time work. Also called *retirement test.*

Equity—In the context of Social Security, equity refers to the relationship between what a person pays in and what he or she is entitled to collect. In a program with perfect equity, benefits would be determined solely on the basis of what a person paid in. If people who have paid a small amount into the fund can collect proportionately more than those who have paid a great deal, the equity of the program is weakened. One of the ongoing arguments over Social Security has been how strong the program's equity should be.

General revenues—that part of the income of the federal government that is not earmarked for a specific purpose. May come from personal income tax, business income tax, excise tax, or other types of government income. Social Security payments are supported by a payroll tax, which is not considered part of general revenues.

HI—health insurance. One of the three main funds of the Social Security program. Pays for Part A of Medicare.

Indexing—the linkage of automatic raises in Social Security benefits to the Consumer Price Index. Also called *cost-of-living increase.*

Level earnings estimate—a basis for predicting the amount of money that the payroll tax will bring into the Social Security fund in future years. It is based on the premise that total wages will remain at a constant level. In the post–World War II years, when the country experienced rapid economic growth, the estimate proved to be too conservative. Also called *level earnings assumption.*

Means test—a requirement that a person show economic need in order to collect benefits from a social welfare program. May be based on annual income, net worth of personal assets, or a combination of these. Social Security retirement benefits require no means test for a person to be eligible to collect.

Minimum benefit—the lowest amount of primary benefit paid to those workers who paid payroll taxes on a low amount of wages or for a short period of time.

OASI—old-age and survivors' insurance. One of the three main funds of the Social Security program. The original Social Security program was entirely OASI.

Payroll tax—a tax on employee wages that pays for the Social Security programs—OASI, DI, and HI. As of 1982, both employee and employer were required to pay tax amounting to 6.7 percent of the first $39,000 of an employee's salary. Self-employed people were required to pay 9.65 percent of their first $39,000 in earned income. The payroll tax is separate from federal income tax, and the money from payroll taxes is to be used only for Social Security.

Replacement rate—a statistic that shows what part of a worker's wage will be replaced by Social Security monthly benefits when he or she retires.

Reserve fund—the repository of payments made from payroll taxes to the Social Security system. Held by the federal government, which pays benefits directly from the established fund. Original Social Security Act set up a single fund, the federal Old Age and Survivors Insurance Fund. Retirement benefits are paid from this fund. With the addition of disability and Medicare benefits to the Social Security program, separate funds were set up for these purposes. Payroll tax is divided among the funds by a percentage schedule set by Congress. Medicare fund also receives separate payments from those electing to participate in some parts of the Medicare program, and from general revenues.

Retirement test—see *earnings limitation.*

Wage base—the maximum amount of yearly wages on which a worker must pay payroll tax to the Social Security system.

FOR FURTHER READING

Ball, Robert M. *Social Security Today and Tomorrow*. New York: Columbia University Press, 1978.

Campbell, Rita Ricardo. *Social Security: Promise and Reality*. Stanford, CA: Hoover Institution Press, Stanford University, 1977.

Derthick, Martha. *Policymaking for Social Security*. Washington, D.C.: The Brookings Institution, 1979.

Myers, Robert J. *Social Security*. Bryn Mawr, Pa: McCahan Foundation, 1975.

Pratt, Henry J. *The Gray Lobby*. Chicago: University of Chicago Press, 1976.

Shore, Warren. *Social Security: The Fraud in Your Future*. New York: Macmillan, 1975.

INDEX

Disability Insurance
(continued)
    added to Social Security program, 22
    eligibility for, 23, 45–46, 48–49, 56
    proposed changes in, 45–46
Disabled people, 1–2
Dole, Senator, 52
"Double dipping," 66–67

Early retirement, 33–34, 47–48, 52, 54, 56
Earnings restrictions. *See* Retirement tests
Eisenhower, President Dwight D., 22
"Elderly lobby," 36, 39

Federal Old-Age and Survivors Insurance Trust Fund, 12
Foley, Representative Thomas, 50
Ford, President Gerald R., 38
Friedman, Milton, 16
Fuller, Ida, 37

General tax revenues, 24, 39, 45–46, 54, 62, 66, 68–69, 72
Gephardt, Representative Richard A., 46
Government employees, 10, 20, 48, 56, 66–67
Government pensions, 48, 56, 66–67
Gradison, Representative Bill, 45

Gray Panthers, *35*
Great Depression, the, 5, *6*, 7, 13
Great Society, the, 24

Health and Human Services, Department of, 47
Health Insurance (HI), 24–26, 31, 45–46, 61–62, 65–66
    eligibility for, 24–26
    See also Medicare
Hoover, President Herbert, 5
House of Representatives, U.S., 47, 50, 56–57
    Select Committee on Aging, 54–56
    Social Security Subcommittee, 45–49, 63
    Ways and Means Committee, 27–28, 39, 62
Humphrey, Vice President Hubert H., *25*

Income tax, personal, 3, 46, 62, 68, 71
Individual Retirement Account (IRA), 72–73
Inflation, 1–2, 32–33, 36, 41, 54, 59, 65, 69, 73

Johnson, President Lyndon B., 24, *25*

Labor unions, 66, 72
Liberals, 32
Life expectancy, 2, 33, 39, 60

Married vs. single tax-
payers, 13
Means tests, 14, 21, 24, 44,
69-71
Medicaid, 24, 44, 56
Medicare program of 1965,
1, 24, *25*, 26–27, 36, 44,
62, 65–66
    amendments to, 24
    eligibility for, 56
Middle class, 13–14
Mills, Representative Wil-
bur, 27–28
Moynihan, Senator Daniel
P., 55
Myers, Robert, 33, 46, 56,
70

National Council of Senior
Citizens, 50
National Council on the
Aging, 50
National Federation of
Independent Businesses,
71
New Deal, the, 5
New York Times, 2, 68
Nixon, President Richard
M., 27–28

Old-Age Assistance (OAA),
8, 13, 16–17, 20
Old Age and Survivors In-
surance (OASI), 24, 31,
45, 61, 65–66
    eligibility for, 8, 10,
    12–13, 16, 22–23, 33,
    39, 45–46, 49, 63–64
O'Neill, Speaker of the
House Thomas P., Jr.,
50

Passell, Peter, 68
Payroll taxes, 8, 10–14, 16–
17, 19–22, 24, 26, 39, 46–
47, 52, 54–55, 57, 59, 61,
66–68, 71
Perkins, Frances, 7, *9*
Pickle, Representative J. J.,
45–46, 50, 66
Poverty level, 36
Presidential campaign of
1980, 39, 41, 43
Private insurance/pension
plans, 14, 16, 20, 36–37,
63–64, 69–73
Progressive Party, 7

Railroad Retirement Act,
10
Reagan, President Ronald,
3, 12, 14, 41, 43–50, 52–
60, 62–64, 67–70
Regressive taxes, 11, 14
Replacement rate, 38, 47
Republican Congressional
Campaign Committee,
57
Republican Party, 22, 27–
28, 39, 45, 52, 55, 57, 60
Retirement tests, 41, 43, 45,
47–48, 53, 69–71
Rivlin, Alice M., 61
Roosevelt, President Frank-
lin D., 5, 7–8, *9*, 11–12,
14, 23, 46, 73–74

"Safety net," 44, 50
Save Our Security Coali-
tion, 50
Schweiker, Secretary Rich-
ard, 47, 49, 52, 54, 66
Self-employed people, 10